SPARROWS SINGING: DISCOVERING ADDITION AND SUBTRACTION

by Megan Atwood

illustrated by Sharon Holm

Content Consultant: Paula J. Maida, PhD

magic wagon

VISIT US AT
WWW.ABDOPUBLISHING.COM

Published by Magic Wagon, a division of the ABDO Group, PO Box 398166, Minneapolis, MN 55439. Copyright © 2012 by Abdo Consulting Group, Inc. International copyrights reserved in all countries. All rights reserved. No part of this book may be reproduced in any form without written permission from the publisher.

Looking Glass Library™ is a trademark and logo of Magic Wagon.

Printed in the United States of America, North Mankato, Minnesota.
102011
012012

♻ THIS BOOK CONTAINS AT LEAST 10% RECYCLED MATERIALS.

Text by Megan Atwood
Illustrations by Sharon Holm
Edited by Lisa Owings
Interior layout by Kazuko Collins
Cover design by Christa Schneider

Library of Congress Cataloging-in-Publication Data

Atwood, Megan.
  Sparrows singing : discovering addition and subtraction / by Megan Atwood ; illustrated by Sharon Lane Holm.
    p. cm. — (Count the critters)
  ISBN 978-1-61641-856-4
  1. Addition—Juvenile literature. 2. Subtraction—Juvenile literature. I. Holm, Sharon Lane, ill. II. Title.
  QA115.A89 2012
  513.2'11—dc23
                              2011033078

Addition is fun! Let's add the

sparrows singing in the bushes.

To add sparrows, count the

sparrows as they join their friends.

The sign to add something

is a plus sign: +.

Let's try it!

Sparrows fly and flutter. They stay low to the ground to find food. Five sparrows land in a bush. Three more fly over to play. To add three to five, count three more sparrows after five: six, seven, eight. $5 + 3 = 8$. Eight sparrows have come to the bush.

1 2 3 4 5 6 7 8 9 10 11 12 13

Sparrows flutter and fly. They don't weigh much. They have hollow bones. This makes it easy for them to fly. Eight sparrows flutter around the bushes. Two more come to play. To add two to eight, count two more sparrows after eight: nine, ten. 8 + 2 = 10. Ten sparrows have come to the bush.

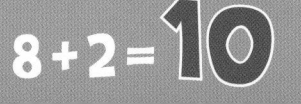

$8 + 2 = 10$

Sparrows chirp and chatter. They have
a high-pitched song. Ten sparrows
chirp to each other in the bush. Four
more sparrows come to chirp, too!

To add four to ten, count four more sparrows after ten: eleven, twelve, thirteen, fourteen. 10 + 4 = 14. Fourteen sparrows are singing!

Sparrows chatter and chirp. Fourteen sparrows chatter with each other. Six more join the group. To add six to fourteen, count six more sparrows after fourteen: fifteen, sixteen, seventeen, eighteen, nineteen, twenty. 14 + 6 = 20. Twenty sparrows are singing!

14 15 16 17 18 19 20   14+6=20

Now it's time to learn subtraction!
To subtract sparrows, take away the
sparrows that fly somewhere else.
The sign to subtract something
is a minus sign: -.
Let's try it!

Sparrows dust and dance. Sparrows take baths in the dust! Two of the twenty sparrows leave the bush. They fly to the dust to take a bath. To subtract two from twenty, take away two sparrows: nineteen, eighteen. $20 - 2 = 18$. Eighteen sparrows are left in the bush!

8 7 6 5 4 3 2 1   20−2=**18**

Sparrows dance and dust. Sparrows wiggle in the dust and flap their wings. Four more sparrows leave the bush. They start to dance in the dirt.

To subtract four from eighteen, take away four sparrows: seventeen, sixteen, fifteen, fourteen. 18 – 4 = 14. Fourteen sparrows are left in the bush!

8 7 6 5 4 3 2 1   18 – 4 = 14

Sparrows flock and friend. Sparrows like to take baths with friends. They smooth their feathers when they're done. Three more sparrows leave the bush.

They flock to the dust. To subtract three from fourteen, take away three sparrows: thirteen, twelve, eleven. 14 – 3 = 11. Eleven sparrows are left in the bush!

8 7 6 5 4 3 2 1   14 – 3 = 11

Sparrows friend and flock. They eat seeds, grass, and bugs with friends. Five more sparrows leave the bush. To subtract five from eleven, take away five sparrows: ten, nine, eight, seven, six. $11 - 5 = 6$. Six sparrows are left in the bush!

Sparrows fly and flutter, chirp and chatter, dust and dance, and flock and friend. Sparrows are busy. They like to fly together! Sparrows come and go all day long. Now you know how to add and subtract!

Words to Know

dust—to take a dirt bath.

flap—to move up and down.

flock—to come together in a group.

flutter—to flap the wings quickly.

hollow—empty inside.

wiggle—to make short, quick movements from side to side or up and down.

Web Sites

To learn more about addition and subtraction, visit ABDO Group online at **www.abdopublishing.com**. Web sites about addition and subtraction are featured on our Book Links page. These links are routinely monitored and updated to provide the most current information available.

1 2 3 4 5 6 7 8 9 **10** 11 **12** 13 **14** 15 **16** 17 **18** 19 **20**